Don't Stop Dreaming, Abby

Written by Milena A. Nemecio

Illustrated by Sarah K. Turner

Halo
PUBLISHING
INTERNATIONAL

Don't Stop Dreaming, Abby
Copyright © 2021 Milena A. Nemecio
Illustrated by Sarah K. Turner
All rights reserved.

ISBN: 978-1-61244-951-7
LCCN: 2020924617

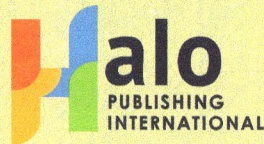

Halo Publishing International, LLC
8000 W Interstate 10, Suite 600
San Antonio, Texas 78230
www.halopublishing.com

Printed and bound in the United States of America

To my husband Pedro, and my dog, Koda,
for your love and support.

To my little sister Keila,
don't stop following your dreams.

To my family for your care and love.

Abby's dreams were big, fun and sometimes a little too rowdy. She told stories beyond anyone's wildest imagination. She played, laughed and acted silly to make others smile—a bit too much.

"Abby, pay attention," the teacher would say.

"Oops, sorry!"

Trying to focus in school was always a challenge. Abby could hardly pay attention. As soon as the teacher started the lesson, Abby noticed Sammy had new shoes or how the clock made a faint ticking sound as she counted the seconds. Then her eyes shifted to the window.

As she stared at the great outdoors, she saw herself racing through the tall grass and jumping high over any obstacle. She imagined being in a race as she crossed the finish line. When an airplane flew overhead, she pictured herself flying at great heights seeing the world and its wonders.

"Abby!" said her teacher. Giggles filled the room.

"Sorry," Abby said.

"Why don't you pay attention? You're so distracted. Don't be lazy, Abby," her parents repeated to her every day. "Why can't you be good?"

"I don't know. I want to. I really do," Abby said, biting her lip.

Abby had trouble making friends at school, and when she did, it was hard for her to keep them. The other kids thought she was weird. She often said things completely different from what the group was talking about.

Sometimes she said things that others didn't like. It made other kids not want to talk or play with her.

She'd try to apologize. "Oh, I didn't mean to say that. It sounded different and good in my head."

But her classmates didn't listen.

Her room was never tidy. She wasn't lazy, but she couldn't stay organized. Mommy would often scold her. She forgot where she put her shoes which made her late for school. She would misplace her backpack and homework and got in trouble in class.

Abby began to dislike school. No one wanted to play with her. The teacher often described her as smart but disruptive. She told Abby that she would do much better if she stopped daydreaming, paid attention and did her work.

Her report cards weren't excellent, like her sister's. She wished she could be smart like her.

Her sister got rewards; Abby got punished.

She began to feel different. She began to feel alone. She wondered why everything was so easy for her sister and all the other kids. She wanted to be like them. She wished she could fit in.

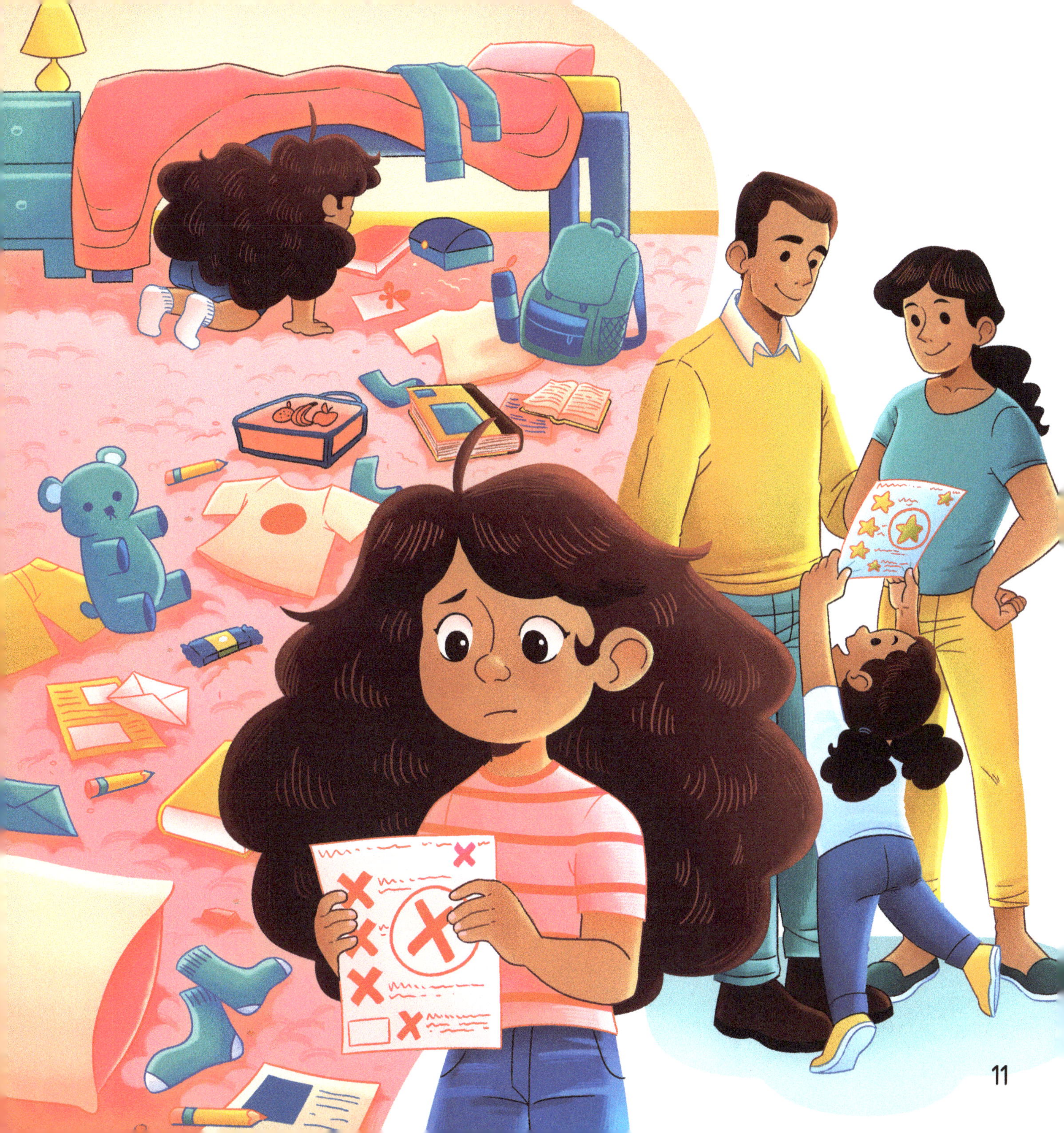

One day she was sent to meet a different teacher at school. Abby was nervous because she thought she was in trouble again.

But when she entered the room, she saw a lady sitting in a chair with a warm and welcoming smile.

Her name was Ms. Robinson, and she said she was there to help Abby.

Ms. Robinson sat Abby in a chair, and they talked for a few minutes. Then Ms. Robinson began to ask questions, telling Abby to respond the best she could.

"Do you like school?" she asked.

"Sometimes," Abby said.

"Do you have friends?"

"No."

"How do you feel about not having friends?"

"Lonely."

Finally, Ms. Robinson asked, "Do you think you are smart?"

Abby didn't feel smart at all. "No," she said.

Ms. Robinson moved in close and said to Abby, "You are a smart, sweet and very imaginative little girl."

Ms. Robinson explained that Abby was not a bad child, and she certainly was not dumb. Abby had something called ADHD. ADHD made her forget things, say the wrong things and made her daydream all the time.

"But does that mean I will never be like the other kids, or pay attention, or ever be normal?" Abby asked, really worried.

"No one is normal," Ms. Robinson replied with a sweet voice. "We're all different, each with our own unique traits."

ADHD

"You have ADHD, but that's not going to stop you from reaching your goals. You're small, but don't ever be afraid to face the world and its obstacles. You're different, but don't ever be afraid to be yourself. Your mind is sharp, so don't ever stop creating. Your imagination is lively, so don't ever stop dreaming. You're going to do great things. Don't stop dreaming, Abby."

Ms. Robinson often worked with Abby one-on-one. She gave her fun things to do that kept her busy and helped her learn. They played games with math and science, and soon enough, Abby remembered how to solve problems and find answers.

One day Ms. Robinson pulled her aside and said, "Abby, you're a warrior so strong and kind. I have a quest for you. You have missions to complete here at school and at home. You will do your homework, clean and find what has been lost, and when you feel yourself forgetting which ones to do you will have me to remind you. Your parents know as well. You're not alone, and you will win in the end."

Every day, Abby completed tasks she had never been able to do. She followed routines and did much better in school. She completed every mission she was given. And it felt good to accomplish what had seemed difficult for her before.

As time went on, Abby looked back at what she had done. Each step of the way surprised her, but she was happy that she overcame every obstacle.

Ms. Robinson told her ADHD was not an obstacle, but a different path in her journey of life. She'd proved that she was strong and brave enough to keep going and follow her dreams.

"Don't stop dreaming, Abby!"

www.ingramcontent.com/pod-product-compliance
Lightning Source LLC
LaVergne TN
LVHW070837080426
835509LV00027B/3490

9 781612 449517